Canada

Zoë Dawson

RSVP
RAINTREE
STECK-VAUGHN
PUBLISHERS
The Steck-Vaughn Company

Austin, Texas

Published by Raintree Steck-Vaughn Publishers, an imprint of Steck-Vaughn Company

A ZOË BOOK

Editor: Kath Davies, Helene Resky
Design: Jan Sterling, Sterling Associates
Map: Gecko Limited
Production: Grahame Griffiths

Library of Congress Cataloging-in-Publication Data

Dawson, Zoë.
    Canada / Zoë Dawson.
        p. cm. — (Postcards from)
    Includes index.
    ISBN 0-8172-4014-4 (lib. binding)
    ISBN 0-8172-4235-X (softcover)
    1. Canada — Juvenile literature. [1. Canada.]
    I. Title. II. Series.
    F1008.2.D38 1996
    971–dc20   95–16223
                                                                                          CIP
                                                                                           AC

Printed and bound in the United States
1 2 3 4 5 6 7 8 9 0 WZ 99 98 97 96 95

Photographic acknowledgments

The publishers wish to acknowledge, with thanks, the following photographic sources:

The Hutchison Library / Brian Moser - title page, 20; / Nancy Durrell McKenna 22; / Robert Francis 28; Robert Harding Picture Library 24; / Tim Winter - cover tl; / Tony Waltham 14; Zefa - cover bl & r, 6, 8, 10, 12, 16, 18, 26.

The publishers have made every effort to trace the copyright holders, but if they have inadvertently overlooked any, they will be pleased to make the necessary arrangement at the first opportunity.

Contents

All the words that appear in **bold** are explained in the Glossary on page 30.

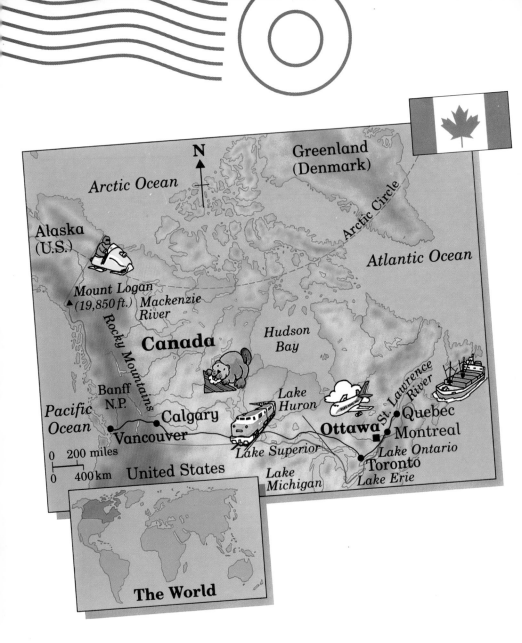

A big map of Canada
and a small map of the world

Dear Tashon,

You can see Canada in red on the small map. It is north of the United States. Canada is one of the biggest countries in the world. Most people live in the south of Canada.

Love,

Esmeralda

P.S. Dad says that Canada is not as big as Russia, but it is bigger than the United States. Ten times as many people live in the United States as live in Canada.

The city of Toronto and Lake Ontario

Dear Betsy,

We are in Toronto. It is the biggest city in Canada. It took about 2 hours for the plane to fly here from Washington, D.C. We saw Lake Ontario from the plane. It is a very big lake!

Your friend,

Rick

P.S. Dad says that Lake Ontario is one of five big lakes called the Great Lakes. Lake Superior is the biggest. It is about the same size as South Carolina!

Jacques Cartier Place, Montreal

Dear Mandy,

We went for a ride in a carriage like this one. The horses went very slowly through the streets of old Montreal. The city is on an island. Mom gave me some Canadian dollars to pay for the ride.

Love,

Jo

P.S. Dad says that Jacques Cartier came to Canada more than 500 years ago. He was the first person to use the name *Canada*.

Old houses in Quebec city

Dear Martin,

You would like Quebec. Most people speak French! Most people speak English, too. Quebec city is the oldest city in Canada. People have lived here for about 500 years.

Yours,

Peter

P.S. Mom says that about a quarter of all Canadians speak French. Most French-speaking Canadians live in the **province** of Quebec.

An Italian restaurant in Vancouver

Dear Jamie,

The food in Canada is good. People cook in many different ways. We go out to eat dinner at **restaurants**. We choose a different one each day. I like Italian food best.

Love,

Kirsty

P.S. Dad says that people from all over the world live in Canada. Some people came from the Ukraine, near Russia. We are going to a Ukrainian restaurant tonight!

A train to Vancouver passing through the Rocky Mountains

Dear Alan,

The road across Canada is about 5,000 miles (8,050 km) long. It is the longest road in the world. The quickest way to travel across Canada is to fly. I would rather go by train.

Yours,

Dave

P.S. Grandma went across Canada on this train. She says the trip took four days. She saw the Rocky Mountains from the **observation car** on the train.

Boats in Vancouver harbor

Dear Jill,

Vancouver is on the west coast of Canada. It is warmer than the east coast, but it is wetter here, too. We are going on a boat trip around the harbor. I hope we see some dolphins.

Love,

Angie

P.S. Mom says that we will go to see some of the tallest trees in the world tomorrow. They are called redwoods. They grow in the mountains near Vancouver.

Canoeing in Banff National Park

Dear Jake,

I have seen an eagle and some bears here in the Rocky Mountains. The wild animals are **protected** in this national park. We are going out in canoes on the lake tomorrow.

Your friend,

Steve

P.S. Uncle Joe says the Rocky Mountains stretch from the far north of Canada into the United States in the south. They form a **barrier** between the west coast and the rest of Canada.

Getting ready for a journey by *skidoo*

Dear Monica,

There is a lot of snow here in winter. In northern Canada the **Inuit** people used sleds pulled by dogs to travel over the snow. Now some people use a *skidoo*, or **snowmobile**, like the one in the picture.

Love,

Mary

P.S. Dad says that the land near the **Arctic Circle** is frozen all year round. It is called the **tundra**.

A family with their homemade boat,
on a lake in the summer

Dear Paul,

We flew north across lakes and forests. Now we are close to the Arctic Circle. Our friends have a house near this lake. There are no roads here. We travel around by boat.

Your friend,

James

P.S. Dad says that it is warm here for about two months in the summer. The schools close, and many families spend the summer in places like this one.

Playing ice hockey in the park

Dear Carlos,

Many people in Canada love to play ice hockey. They get plenty of time to play. The winters are long and cold. Children play soccer and hockey at school. They swim, too.

Love,

Heather

P.S. Mom says that Canadians like to spend time outdoors. In the summer many people go walking, bicycling, and camping.

Horse racing at Calgary

Dear Vita,

This is a special race. Each team of four horses pulls a **chuckwagon**. These wagons were used to take food out to the cowboys. The cowboys looked after cattle on large farms called ranches.

Your brother,

Alex

P.S. Mom says that there are many different **festivals** in Canada. Some festivals are held by the Native American peoples.

The Canadian flag, flying in Vancouver

Dear Alice,

The red leaf in the middle of the flag stands for Canada. It comes from the maple tree, which grows here. The stripes come from a British flag flown by ships.

Love,

Lisa

P.S. Dad says that Great Britain used to rule Canada. Now Canada is a **democracy**. The queen of England is still their queen. Canada is ruled from the **capital** city, Ottawa.

Glossary

Arctic Circle: The frozen lands near the North Pole. A line drawn on maps shows the position of the Arctic Circle.

Barrier: Something that keeps one thing away from another. Mountains can be barriers.

Capital: The town or city where people who rule the country meet

Chuckwagon: A wagon carrying food and things needed to cook

Democracy: A country where all the people choose the leaders they want to run the country

Festival: A time when people celebrate something special. People often dance and sing during a festival.

Inuit: A people who live in and near the Arctic

Observation car: A special car on some trains. It often has a glass roof, so that people can see more outside the train.

Protect: To keep safe from danger. People are not allowed to pick wild plants or to hunt wild animals in national parks.

Province: Part of a country that is like a county or a state

P.S.: This stands for Post Script. A postscript is the part of a card or letter that is added at the end, after the person has signed it.

Restaurant: A place where people go to eat meals. People pay for the food they eat in a restaurant.

Snowmobile: A sled with a motor that carries people over the snow

Tundra: A cold, dry place where trees cannot grow

Index